Understanding God's Love for Us

John 3:16-ESV- "For God so loved the world, that he gave his only Son, that whoever believes in him should not perish but have eternal life.

Pearlie Martin

Introduction

This easy-to-read question and answer study guide will take give us insight and revelation knowledge of God's love for us. It will cause us to go deeper into the biblical scriptures line upon line and precept upon precept. It will walk you out of fear and into God's love and holy boldness.

1 John 4:7.8- Dear friends, let us love one another, for love comes from God. Everyone who loves has been born of God and knows God. 8 **Whoever does not love does not know God, because God is love.**

1.Why are we told to love one another, according to verse above?

____

2.Where does love come from according to verse above?

____

3. What does it mean **when we love others**, according to verse above?

____

4. What does it mean **when we do not love others,** according to verse above?

____

5. God is love. T or F

1Corinthians 13:4-5-Love suffers long and is kind; love does not envy; love does not parade itself, is not puffed up; does not behave rudely, does not seek its own, is not provoked, thinks no evil.

1.List the 9 characterstics of God's love, according to verse above?

____

____

____

____

____

____

____

Psalms 86:5-ESV-For you, O Lord, are good and forgiving, abounding in steadfast love to all who call upon you.

1.What 3 things are the Lord described as according to verse above?

____

____

2.Who does God show these 3 things too according to verse above?

____

1Corithians 13:13-ESV-So now faith, hope, and love abide, these three; but the greatest of these is love.

1.What is the greatest out of faith, hope and love, according to verse above?

____

1 John 4:9,10-NLT-God showed how much he loved us by sending his one and only Son into the world so that we might have eternal life through him. This is real love—not that we loved God, but that he loved us and sent his Son as a sacrifice to take away our sins.

1.How did God show how much he loved us according to verse above?

____

2.What's real love described as according to verse above?

____

1John 4:11-12NLT-Dear friends, since God loved us that much, we surely ought to love each other. 12No one has ever seen God. But if we love each other, God lives in us, and his love is brought to full expression in us.

1.Why should we love each other, according to verse above?

____

2. What does it mean when we love each other, according to verse above?

____

3. How is God's love brought to full expression in us, according to verse above?

____

1 John 4:16-17NLT-We know how much God loves us, and we have put our trust in his love. God is love, and all who live in love live in God, and God lives in them. 17And as we live in God, our love grows more perfect. So, we will not be afraid on the day of judgment, but we can face him with confidence because we live like Jesus here in this world.

1.We can put our trust in God's love because we know how much he loves us? T or F

2.What does it mean when we live in love, according to verse above?

____

3.What happens when we live in God, according to verse above?

____

4.Why don't we have to fear the day of judgement, according to verse above?

____

5. Why will we be able to face God with confidence on the day of judgement according to verse above?

____

1John 4:18,19-NLT-Such love has no fear, because perfect love expels all fear. If we are afraid, it is for fear of punishment, and this shows that we have not fully experienced his perfect love. 19We love each other because he loved us first.

1.What kind of love cast out all fear according to verse above?

____

2.What does it shows when we're afraid of punishment or bad news, according to verse above?

____

3.Why do we love others according to verse above?

____

1John 4:20NLT- If someone says, "I love God," but hates a fellow believer, that person is a liar; for if we don't love people we can see, how can we love God, whom we cannot see? And he has given us this command: Those who love God must also love their fellow believers.

1.What does it mean if someone says I love God but hates his fellow believer according to verse above?

____

2.If we don't love people who we can see, what does it say about God who we can't see, according to verse above?

____

3.What must we do to love God?

____

1.What kind of plans does the Lord have for us

____

____

Psalms 63:3-ESV Because your steadfast love is better than life, my lips will praise you.

1.How is God love described from above verse?

____

John 14:6-ESV- Jesus said to him, "I am the way, and the truth, and the life. No one comes to the Father except through me.

1.What 3 things does Jesus say he is according to verse above?

____

2.How must we come to the Father, according to verse above?

____

Isaiah 54:10-ESV- For the mountains may depart and the hills be removed, but my steadfast love shall not depart from you, and my covenant of peace shall not be removed," says the Lord, who has compassion on you.

1. What does God say about his steadfast love, according to verse above?

____

2. What does God say about his covenant of peace, according to verse above?

____

3. What does the Lord have for us, according to verse above?

____

Romans 12:10-ESV- Be devoted to one another in love. Honor one another above yourselves.

1. What are we called to be devoted to, according to verse above?

____

2. What are we told to do concerning honor? _______________________________

Isaiah 41:13-ESV-For I, the Lord your God, hold your right hand; it is I who say to you, "Fear not, I am the one who helps you."

1. What does God says about our right hand, according to verse above?

____

2. What does God tell us not to do because he will help us, according to verse above?

____

1 John 3:16-ESV-By this we know love, that he laid down his life for us, and we ought to lay down our lives for the brothers.

1.How do we recognize love, according to verse above?

____

2.How are we to show our love to our brothers, according to verse above?

____

1 John 4:16-17NLT-We know how much God loves us, and we have put our trust in his love. God is love, and all who live in love live in God, and God lives in them. 17And as we live in God, our love grows more perfect. So, we will not be afraid on the day of judgment, but we can face him with confidence because we live like Jesus here in this world.

1.We can put our trust in God's love because we know how much he loves us? T or F

2.What does it mean when we live in love, according to verse above?

____

3.What happens when we live in God, according to verse above?

____

4.Why don't we have to fear the day of judgement, according to verse above?

____

5. Why will we be able to face God with confidence on the day of judgement according to verse above?

____

James 5:19ESV-My brothers, if anyone among you wanders from the truth and someone brings him back, let him know that whoever brings back a sinner from his wandering will save his soul from death and will cover a multitude of sins.

1. What 2 things happens when we bring a sinner back to the Lord according to verse above?

____

____

Proverbs 28:13-ESV- Whoever conceals his transgressions will not prosper, but he who confesses and forsakes them will obtain mercy.

1. What happens when we hid our sins according to verse above?

____

2. What happens to those who confess and forsake their transgression or sin, according to verse above?

____

Romans 5:8-ESV-But God shows his love for us in that while we were still sinners, Christ died for us.

1. How did God show his love for us, according to verse above?

____

Psalms 147:3-ESV-He heals the brokenhearted and binds up their wounds.

1. What does God do for the brokenhearted according to verse above?

____

Psalms 86:15-ESV-But you, O Lord, are a God merciful and gracious, slow to anger and abounding in steadfast love and faithfulness.

1.What 5 words describes our Lord God, according form verse above?

____

____

Psalms 118:8ESV-The Lord is on my side; I will not fear. What can man do to me?

1.Why do we not have to fear, according to verse above?

1.____

1John 3:1-ESV-See what kind of love the Father has given to us, that we should be called children of God; and so we are. The reason why the world does not know us is that it did not know him.

1.Why does God called us children of God, according to verse above?

____

Psalms 136:26-ESV-Give thanks to the God of heaven, for his steadfast love endures forever.

1.How long does God love endure, according to verse above?

____

Romans 8:31-ESV-What then shall we say to these things? If God is for us, who can be against us? Since he did not spare even his own Son but gave him up for us all, won't he also give us everything else?

1.Because God is for us, who can be against us, according to verse above?

____

2.Because God did not spare his own son, is there anything else he will not freely give us, according to verse above?

____

1John 4:8-ESV-Anyone who does not love does not know God, because God is love.

1.When we do not love what does it mean according to verse above?

____

Deuteronomy 7:9-ESV-Know therefore that the Lord your God is God, the faithful God who keeps covenant and steadfast love with those who love him and keep his commandments, to a thousand generations,

1.Who does our faithful God keep covenant with and shows his steadfast love toward, according to verse above?

____

2.How many generations does he keep his commandments with, according to verse above?

____

Lamentation 3:22,23-ESV-The steadfast love of the Lord never ceases; his mercies never come to an end; they are new every morning; great is your faithfulness.

1.What does the verse says about God steadfast love from verse above?

____

2.What 2 things does the verse above, about God's mercies?

____

____

Romans 5:3-5-ESV-More than that, we rejoice in our sufferings, knowing that suffering produces endurance, and endurance produces character, and character produces hope, and hope does not put us to shame, because God's love has been poured into our hearts through the Holy Spirit who has been given to us.

1.Why should we rejoice in our sufferings according to verse above?

____

____

2.According to verse above, hope does not do what?

____

3. Who has poured the love of God into our hearts according to verse above?

____

Romans 10:13-ESV- For "everyone who calls on the name of the Lord will be saved."

1.How can we be saved according to verse above?

____

Isiah 53:5-ESV- But he was wounded for our transgressions; he was crushed for our iniquities; upon him was the chastisement that brought us peace, and with his stripes we are healed.

1.Why was Jesus wounded according to verse above?

____

2.Why was Jesus Crushed according to verse above?

____

3.What happened to Jesus to cause us to have peace, according to verse above?

____

4. How did Jesus heal us, according to verse above?

____

Romans 8:28-ESV- And we know that for those who love God all things work together for good, for those who are called according to his purpose.

1.What does God cause to happen for those who love him and are called according to his purpose from verse above?

____

Psalms 103:13-ESV- As a father shows compassion to his children, so the Lord shows compassion to those who fear him.

1.How does God shows his compassion for his children, according to verse above?

____

2.Who does the Lord shows compassion to according to verse above?

____

**Revelation 21:3-4-ESV- And I heard a loud voice from the throne saying,
"Behold, the dwelling place of God is with man. He will dwell with them, and
they will be his people and God himself will be with them as their God 4He
will wipe away every tear from their eyes, and death shall be no more, neither
shall there be mourning, nor crying, nor pain anymore, for the former things
have passed away."**

1.Where is God's dwelling place according to verse above?

____

2. Are we consider God's people according to verse above?

____

3.What has God promised to do with our tears, according to verse above?

____

4.What happens to death, mourning, crying, pain according to verse above?

____

5.What happens to the former things according to verse above?

____

**Psalms 35:7-ESV- How precious is your steadfast love, O God! The children of
mankind take refuge in the shadow of your wings**

1.How is God's love described from verse above?

____

2.Where does the children of mankind take refuge in God, according to verse
above?

____

Jeremiah 29:11-ESV- For I know the plans I have for you, declares the Lord, plans for welfare and not for evil, to give you a future and a hope.

1.What's God's plan for us according to verse above?

____

____

John 15:9-7-ESV- As the Father has loved me, so have I loved you. Abide in my love. If you keep my commandments, you will abide in my love, just as I have kept my Father's commandments and abide in his love. These things I have spoken to you, that my joy may be in you, and that your joy may be full. "This is my commandment, that you love one another as I have loved you. Greater love has no one than this, that someone lay down his life for his friends

1.Why do we love others, according to verse above?

____

2.How do we abide in God's love, according to verse above?

____

3.Why does Jesus tells us to abide in his love, according to verse above?

____

4.What is Jesus Commandment to us, according to verse above?

____

5.How did Jesus show his greatest love to us, according to verse above?

____

Psalms 63:3-ESV- Because your steadfast love is better than life, my lips will praise you.

1.Why should our lips praise the Lord, according to verse above?

____

John 14:6-ESV- Jesus said to him, "I am the way, and the truth, and the life. No one comes to the Father except through me.

1.Who is Jesus according to verse above?

____

2. How must we come to Jesus, according to verse above?

____

Isaiah 41:13-ESV- For I, the Lord your God, hold your right hand; it is I who say to you, "Fear not, I am the one who helps you."

1.What does God say he holds, according to verse above?

____

2.What does God says to us according to verse above?

____

Isaiah 54:4-ESV- For the mountains may depart and the hills be removed, but my steadfast love shall not depart from you, and my covenant of peace shall not be removed," says the Lord, who has compassion on you.

1.What is God's promise to us concerning his steadfast love, according to verse above?

____

2.What's God's promise to us concerning his covenant of peace?

____

3. Does God have compassion on us? Y or N

1John 3:16-ESV- By this we know love, that he laid down his life for us, and we ought to lay down our lives for the brothers.

1.How do we know Love, according to verse above?

____

2. What are we to do for our brothers?

____

Psalms 139:14-ESV- I praise you, for I am fearfully and wonderfully made. Wonderful are your works; my soul knows it very well.

1.How did God make us according to verse above?

____

1Corinthians 13:1-3NLT-If I speak in the tongues of men and of angels, but have not love, I am a noisy gong or a clanging cymbal. And if I have prophetic powers, and understand all mysteries and all knowledge, and if I have all faith, so as to remove mountains, but have not love, I am nothing. If I give away all I have, and if I deliver up my body to be burned, but have not love, I gain nothing. Love is patient and kind; love does not envy or boast; it is not arrogant or rude. It does not insist on its own way; it is not irritable or resentful;

1.If we speak with tongues of men and angels but have not love, what are described as, according to verse above?

____

2.What 4 things are mention from above verse which says we are nothing if we have not love?

____

____

____

Psalms 62:8-ESV-Trust in him at all times, O people; pour out your heart before him; God is a refuge for us. Selah

1.What 2 things are we told to do in the Lord, according to verse above?

____

____

2.Who is God to us according to verse above? _____________________________

1John 4:18ESV-There is no fear in love, but perfect love casts out fear. For fear has to do with punishment, and whoever fears has not been perfected in love.

1.What cast out the spirit of fear in our lives, according to verse above?

____

2. What does fear have to do with, according to verse above?

____

3.When we fear, what does it mean, according to verse above?

____

John 13:34-35-ESV-A new commandment I give to you, that you love one another: just as I have loved you, you also are to love one another. By this all people will know that you are my disciples, if you have love for one another."

1.What new commandment has God given us, according to verse above?

____

____

2.When we love one another as disciples, according to verse above?

____

Ephesians 5:25-ESV-Husbands, love your wives, as Christ loved the church and gave himself up for her,

1.How are husbands to love their wives, according to verse above?

1Peter 4:8-ESV-Above all, keep loving one another earnestly, since love covers a multitude of sins.

1.What does God earnestly tell us to do, according to verse above?

Proverbs 8:7-ESV-I love those who love me, and those who seek me diligently find me.

1.Who does God says he love according to verse above?

2.What happens when we seek God diligently, according to verse above?

Behold, I have engraved you on the palms of my hands; your walls are continually before me.

1.Where does God have us engraved, according to verse above?

Colossians 3:14-ESV-And above all these put +on love, which binds everything together in perfect harmony.

1.What binds us together in perfect harmony, according to verse above?

Hebrew 12:6-ESV-For the Lord disciplines the one he loves, and chastises every son whom he receives."

1.Who does the Lord disciplines according to verse above?

____

2.Who does the Lord chastises, according to verse above?

____

Proverbs 10:12-ESV-Hatred stirs up strife, but love covers all offenses.

1.What stirs up strife according to verse above?

____

2.What covers offenses, according to verse above?

____

Hebrew 13:5ESV- Keep your life free from love of money, and be content with what you have, for he has said, "I will never leave you nor forsake you."

1.What does God tell us to do about money, according to verse above?

____

____

2.How does God tell us to be?

____

3.What has God promised to never do to us, according to verse above?

____

____

2 Corinthian 5:21-ESV- For our sake he made him to be sin who knew no sin, so that in him we might become the righteousness of God.

1.Why did God make Jesus to be sin according to verse above?

____

HEBREW 12:6ESV- For the Lord disciplines the one he loves, and chastises every son whom he receives."

1.Who does the Lord disciplines, according to verse above?

____

____

2.Who does the Lord chastise, according to verse above?

____

Romans 6:23-ESV-For the wages of sin is death, but the free gift of God is eternal life in Christ Jesus our Lord.

1.What's the wages of sin, according to verse above?

____

2.What is God's free gift to us, according to verse above?

____

____

John 10:9-11-ESV- I am the door. If anyone enters by me, he will be saved and will go in and out and find pasture. The thief comes only to steal and kill and destroy. I came that they may have life and have it abundantly. I am the good shepherd. The good shepherd lays down his life for the sheep.

1.Who's the door according to verse above?

2. What happens when we enter into the door or accept Jesus, according to verse above?

3.What 3 things does the thief come to do according to verse above?

4. What did Jesus comes to do, according to verse above?

5.What did Jesus the good shepherd come to do according to verse above?

Matthew 11:28-30-ESV-Come to me, all who labor and are heavy laden, and I will give you rest. Take my yoke upon you, and learn from me, for I am gentle and lowly in heart, and you will find rest for your souls. For my yoke is easy, and my burden is light."

1.What does Jesus promise all those who labor and are heavy laden?

____

2.What has Jesus promised to do for us when we take his yoke upon us and learn from him, according to verse above?

____

3.What does Jesus tell us about his yoke and his burden according to verse above?

____

1John 4:10-ESV-In this is love, not that we have loved God but that he loved us and sent his Son to be the propitiation for our sins.

1.Why did God send his son, according to verse above?

____

Psalms 147:7ESV-He heals the brokenhearted and binds up their wounds.

1.What 2 things did Jesus do for us, according to verse above?

____

____

Proverbs 10:12-ESV-Hatred stirs up strife, but love covers all offenses.

1.What stirs up strife according to verse above?

2.What covers all offenses, according to verse above?

Hebrews 13:4-ESV-Keep your life free from love of money, and be content with what you have, for he has said, "I will never leave you nor forsake you."

1.What are we told to keep our life free from, according to verse above?

2.What are we told to be content with, according to verse above?

3.What has God promised to do for us, according to verse above?

Matthew 22:37-39-ESV-And he said to him, "You shall love the Lord your God with all your heart and with all your soul and with all your mind. This is the great and first commandment. And a second is like it: You shall love your neighbor as yourself.

1.According to the first commandment, how are we to Love the Lord our God, according to verse above?

2.How are we to love our neighbor according to verse above?

1 Corinthians 16:14-ESV-Let all that you do be done in love

1.How are we to do things, according to verse above?

____

John 14:15-ESV- "If you love me, you will keep my commandments.

1.How do we show that we love Jesus, according to verse above?

____

1Corinthians 13:8-ESV-Love never ends. As for prophecies, they will pass away; as for tongues, they will cease; as for knowledge, it will pass away.

1.What will never end according to verse above?

____

Proverbs 3:3.4-ESV-Let not steadfast love and faithfulness forsake you; bind them around your neck; write them on the tablet of your heart. So, you will find favor and good success in the sight of God and man.

1.What are we not to forsake according to verse above?

____

____

2.What 2 things are we to bind around our neck according to verse above?

____

3.What 2 things are we to write on the tablet of our hearts, according to verse above?

____

____

John 3:36-ESV-Whoever believes in the Son has eternal life; whoever does not obey the Son shall not see life, but the wrath of God remains on him.

1. What happens for those who believes in the Son, according to verse above?

____

____

2. What 2 things happens to those who does not obey the Son, according to verse above?

____

____

Isaiah 53:6ESV-All we like sheep have gone astray; we have turned—every one—to his own way; and the Lord has laid on him the iniquity of us all.

1. Why did the Lord have our iniquity laid upon himself, according to verse above?

____

2. What did the Lord laid down his iniquity for us all, according to verse above?

____

Psalms 46:1-ESV-God is our refuge and strength, always ready to help in times of trouble.

1. Who is God described as according to verse above?

____

2. What does God do in our times of troubles according to verse above?

____

Galatians 5:22-23-ESV-But the fruit of the Spirit is love, joy, peace, patience, kindness, goodness, faithfulness, gentleness, self-control; against such things there is no law.

1. What are the nine fruits of the Spirit, according to verse above?

____

____

____

____

____

____

____

____

1John 4:12-ESV-No one has ever seen God; if we love one another, God abides in us and his love is perfected in us.

1. What happens when we love each other according to verse above?

____

2 Thessalonians 3:5-ESV-May the Lord direct your hearts to the love of God and to the steadfastness of Christ.

1. What can the Lord direct our hearts toward when we pray, according to verse above?

____

Acts 4:12-ESV-And there is salvation in no one else, for there is no other name under heaven given among men by which we must be saved."

1.What name under heaven must we be saved?

Psalms 103:2-5-ESV-Bless the Lord, O my soul, and forget not all his benefits, who forgives all your iniquity, who heals all your diseases, who redeems your life from the pit, who crowns you with steadfast love and mercy, who satisfies v with good so that your youth is renewed like the eagle's.

1.List the 5 benefits of the Lord, according to verse above?

Romans 12:9ESV-Let love be genuine. Abhor what is evil; hold fast to what is good.

1.What kind of love are we told to have, according to verse above?

2.What are we supposed to do with evil, according to verse above?

3.What are we to hold fast to, according to verse above?

For answer key, please email us at Pearliepublishing@gmail.com and please write the words answer key and the name of your book in the subject line of the email.

Follow us on Facebook at Pearlie Martin books